# The Walk of Faith Journals

## Building Your Faith Daily

## Volume 2

## April, May, June

Brenda Williams

The Walk of Faith Journals, Volume 2
Copyright © 2022 Brenda Williams

Scripture quotations marked KJV are taken from the King James Version of the Bible, Public Domain. Scripture quotations marked NIV are taken from the Holy Bible, New International Version®, NIV® Copyright ©2011 by Biblica, Inc.® Used by permission. All rights reserved worldwide. "Scripture quotations marked ESV are from the ESV® Bible (The Holy Bible, English Standard Version®), Copyright © 2001 by Crossway, a publishing ministry of Good News Publishers. Used by permission. All rights reserved.

All rights reserved under International Copyright Law. No part of this journal may be reproduced or transmitted in any form or by any means without written permission of the Publisher, except for the inclusion of brief quotations in a review.

Monthly Reflections by Burdetta Thomas

Cover designs by Anita Jackson


Published by:
Brenda Williams
Suitland, MD

Published in the United States of America.

ISBN 978-0-578-39140-3

# APRIL

# *Salvation*

## THE WALK OF FAITH JOURNALS
*Building Your Faith Daily*

### Book 4

### Brenda Williams

# APRIL

Book 4 in The Walk of Faith Journals

## Salvation

This Journal will give you a Scripture every day to read, meditate, and memorize. Read the Scripture three times a day. Ask the Holy Spirit to help you memorize the Scripture and give you revelation on His Word.

## REFLECTION

## *Salvation*

You sought me out in the muck and mire. Your goal was to reconcile and redeem me. All I had to do was acknowledge my own wickedness and sin. Then confess that Jesus is Lord. You cleansed me and washed me clean. You forgot every dirty deed and promised to remember no more. You gave me clean hands, clear conscience, and a clean heart. With a fresh start I can navigate through this sin-sick world and live holy, clothed in Your righteousness. I now have real joy and real peace. Thank You for saving me from myself. I have been saved to truly live again!

# DAY 1  Date_____

Acts 4:12 (NIV)
Salvation is found in no one else, for there is no other name under heaven given to mankind by which we must be saved.

In your own words, write what this Scripture means to you.
_____
_____
_____
_____
_____
_____

How can you apply this Scripture to your life today?
_____
_____
_____
_____
_____
_____

What have you prayed for and you received it immediately after you prayed?
_____
_____
_____
_____
_____

Pray for 15 - 30 minutes and write any thoughts the Holy Spirit brings to your mind.

_____
_____
_____
_____
_____
_____
_____
_____

Today I will

_____
_____
_____
_____
_____
_____
_____
_____
_____
_____
_____
_____
_____
_____

# DAY 2

Date_____

Acts 16:31 (NIV)
They replied, "Believe in the Lord Jesus, and you will be saved—you and your household."

In your own words, write what this Scripture means to you.

_____
_____
_____
_____
_____
_____

How can you apply this Scripture to your life today?

_____
_____
_____
_____
_____
_____

What have you prayed for and you received it immediately after you prayed?

_____
_____
_____
_____
_____
_____

Pray for 15 - 30 minutes and write any thoughts the Holy Spirit brings to your mind.

Today I will

# DAY 3

Date_____

Psalm 62:1 (NIV)
Truly my soul finds rest in God; my salvation comes from him.

In your own words, write what this Scripture means to you.

_____
_____
_____
_____
_____
_____

How can you apply this Scripture to your life today?

_____
_____
_____
_____
_____
_____

What have you prayed for and you received it immediately after you prayed?

_____
_____
_____
_____
_____
_____

Pray for 15 - 30 minutes and write any thoughts the Holy Spirit brings to your mind.

___

Today I will

___

# DAY 4

Date_____

Acts 2:21 (NIV)
And anyone who calls on the name of the Lord will be saved.

In your own words, write what this Scripture means to you.

_____
_____
_____
_____
_____
_____

How can you apply this Scripture to your life today?

_____
_____
_____
_____
_____
_____

What have you prayed for and you received it immediately after you prayed?

------------------------------------------------------------
------------------------------------------------------------
------------------------------------------------------------
------------------------------------------------------------
------------------------------------------------------------
------------------------------------------------------------

Pray for 15 - 30 minutes and write any thoughts the Holy Spirit brings to your mind.

_____
_____
_____
_____
_____
_____
_____

Today I will

_____
_____
_____
_____
_____
_____
_____
_____
_____
_____
_____
_____
_____
_____

# DAY 5         Date_____

Romans 10:10 (NIV)
For it is with your heart that you believe and are justified, and it is with your mouth that you profess your faith and are saved.

In your own words, write what this Scripture means to you.

_____
_____
_____
_____
_____
_____

How can you apply this Scripture to your life today?

_____
_____
_____
_____
_____

What have you prayed for and you received it immediately after you prayed?

_____
_____
_____
_____
_____
_____

Pray for 15 - 30 minutes and write any thoughts the Holy Spirit brings to your mind.

_____
_____
_____
_____
_____
_____
_____

Today I will

_____
_____
_____
_____
_____
_____
_____
_____
_____
_____
_____
_____
_____
_____

# DAY 6                           Date_____

Titus 2: 11-12 (NIV)

For the grace of God has appeared that offers salvation to all people. It teaches us to say "No" to ungodliness and worldly passions, and to live self-controlled, upright and godly lives in this present age.

In your own words, write what this Scripture means to you.

_____
_____
_____
_____
_____
_____

How can you apply this Scripture to your life today?

_____
_____
_____
_____
_____
_____

What have you prayed for and you received it immediately after you prayed?

_____
_____
_____
_____
_____
_____

Pray for 15 - 30 minutes and write any thoughts the Holy Spirit brings to your mind.

_____
_____
_____
_____
_____
_____
_____
_____

Today I will

_____
_____
_____
_____
_____
_____
_____
_____
_____
_____
_____
_____
_____
_____

# DAY 7

Date_____

Luke 19:10 (NIV)

For the Son of Man came to seek and to save the lost.

In your own words, write what this Scripture means to you.

_____
_____
_____
_____
_____
_____

How can you apply this Scripture to your life today?

_____
_____
_____
_____
_____

What have you prayed for and you received it immediately after you prayed?

_____
_____
_____
_____
_____

Pray for 15 - 30 minutes and write any thoughts the Holy Spirit brings to your mind.

___

Today I will

___

# DAY 8

Date_____

2 Peter 3:9 (NIV)
The Lord is not slow in keeping His promise, as some understand slowness. Instead He is patient with you, not wanting anyone to perish, but everyone to come to repentance.

In your own words, write what this Scripture means to you.

_____
_____
_____
_____
_____
_____

How can you apply this Scripture to your life today?

_____
_____
_____
_____
_____
_____

What have you prayed for and you received it immediately after you prayed?

_____
_____
_____
_____
_____
_____

Pray for 15 - 30 minutes and write any thoughts the Holy Spirit brings to your mind.

Today I will

# DAY 9

Date_____

Mark 16:16 (NIV)
Whoever believes and is baptized will be saved, but whoever does not believe will be condemned.

In your own words, write what this Scripture means to you.

_____
_____
_____
_____
_____
_____

How can you apply this Scripture to your life today?

_____
_____
_____
_____
_____
_____

What have you prayed for and you received it immediately after you prayed?

_____
_____
_____
_____
_____
_____

Pray for 15 - 30 minutes and write any thoughts the Holy Spirit brings to your mind.

_____

Today I will

_____

# DAY 10             Date_____

1 Peter 1:8-9 (NIV)

Though you have not seen Him, you love Him; and even though you do not see Him now, you believe in Him and are filled with an inexpressible and glorious joy, for you are receiving the end result of your faith, the salvation of your souls.

In your own words, write what this Scripture means to you.

_____
_____
_____
_____
_____
_____

How can you apply this Scripture to your life today?

_____
_____
_____
_____
_____
_____

What have you prayed for and you received it immediately after you prayed?

-----------------------------------------------
-----------------------------------------------
-----------------------------------------------
-----------------------------------------------
-----------------------------------------------

Pray for 15 - 30 minutes and write any thoughts the Holy Spirit brings to your mind.

_____
_____
_____
_____
_____
_____
_____

Today I will

_____
_____
_____
_____
_____
_____
_____
_____
_____
_____
_____
_____
_____
_____

# DAY 11

Date_____

Hebrews 9:28 (NIV)

So Christ was sacrificed once to take away the sins of many; and He will appear a second time, not to bear sin, but to bring salvation to those who are waiting for Him.

In your own words, write what this Scripture means to you.

_____
_____
_____
_____
_____

How can you apply this Scripture to your life today?

_____
_____
_____
_____
_____

What have you prayed for and you received it immediately after you prayed?

_____
_____
_____
_____
_____
_____

Pray for 15 - 30 minutes and write any thoughts the Holy Spirit brings to your mind.

_____
_____
_____
_____
_____
_____
_____

Today I will

-----------------------------------------------
-----------------------------------------------
-----------------------------------------------
-----------------------------------------------
-----------------------------------------------
-----------------------------------------------
-----------------------------------------------
_____
_____
_____
_____
_____
_____
_____

# DAY 12     Date_____

Romans 1:16 (NIV)

For I am not ashamed of the gospel, because it is the power of God that brings salvation to everyone who believes, first to the Jew, then to the Gentile.

In your own words, write what this Scripture means to you.

_____
_____
_____
_____
_____
_____

How can you apply this Scripture to your life today?

_____
_____
_____
_____
_____
_____

What have you prayed for and you received it immediately after you prayed?

_____
_____
_____
_____
_____
_____

Pray for 15 - 30 minutes and write any thoughts the Holy Spirit brings to your mind.

_____
_____
_____
_____
_____
_____
_____
_____

Today I will

_____
_____
_____
_____
_____
_____
_____
_____
_____
_____
_____
_____
_____
_____

# DAY 13    Date_____

Romans 5:10 (NIV)
For if, while we were God's enemies, we were reconciled to Him through the death of His Son, how much more, having been reconciled, shall we be saved through His life?

In your own words, write what this Scripture means to you.

_____
_____
_____
_____
_____
_____

How can you apply this Scripture to your life today?

_____
_____
_____
_____
_____
_____

What have you prayed for and you received it immediately after you prayed?

-----------------------------------------------
-----------------------------------------------
-----------------------------------------------
-----------------------------------------------
-----------------------------------------------
-----------------------------------------------

Pray for 15 - 30 minutes and write any thoughts the Holy Spirit brings to your mind.

_____
_____
_____
_____
_____
_____
_____
_____

Today I will

_____
_____
_____
_____
_____
_____
_____
_____
_____
_____
_____
_____
_____
_____
_____

# DAY 14

Date_____

John 3:17 (NIV)
For God did not send His Son into the world to condemn the world, but to save the world through Him.

In your own words, write what this Scripture means to you.

_____
_____
_____
_____
_____
_____

How can you apply this Scripture to your life today?

_____
_____
_____
_____
_____

What have you prayed for and you received it immediately after you prayed?

_____
_____
_____
_____
_____
_____

Pray for 15 - 30 minutes and write any thoughts the Holy Spirit brings to your mind.

_____
_____
_____
_____
_____
_____
_____
_____

Today I will

_____
_____
_____
_____
_____
_____
_____
_____
_____
_____
_____
_____
_____
_____

# DAY 15

Date_____

Psalm 62:7 (NIV)

My salvation and my honor depend on God; He is my mighty rock, my refuge.

In your own words, write what this Scripture means to you.

_____
_____
_____
_____
_____
_____

How can you apply this Scripture to your life today?

_____
_____
_____
_____
_____
_____

What have you prayed for and you received it immediately after you prayed?

_____
_____
_____
_____
_____
_____

Pray for 15 - 30 minutes and write any thoughts the Holy Spirit brings to your mind.

___

Today I will

___

# DAY 16

Date_____

Ephesians 2:8-9 (NIV)

For it is by grace you have been saved, through faith—and this is not from yourselves, it is the gift of God—not only by works, so that no one can boast.

In your own words, write what this Scripture means to you.

_____
_____
_____
_____
_____
_____

How can you apply this Scripture to your life today?

_____
_____
_____
_____
_____
_____

What have you prayed for and you received it immediately after you prayed?

_____
_____
_____
_____
_____
_____

Pray for 15 - 30 minutes and write any thoughts the Holy Spirit brings to your mind.

___

Today I will

___

# DAY 17                    Date_____

John 3:16 (NIV)
For God so loved the world that He gave his one and only Son, that whoever believes in Him shall not perish but have eternal life.

In your own words, write what this Scripture means to you.

_____
_____
_____
_____
_____
_____

How can you apply this Scripture to your life today?

_____
_____
_____
_____
_____

What have you prayed for and you received it immediately after you prayed?

_____
_____
_____
_____
_____
_____

Pray for 15 - 30 minutes and write any thoughts the Holy Spirit brings to your mind.

Today I will

# DAY 18

Date_____

Hebrews 7:25 (NIV)
Therefore He is able to save completely those who come to God through Him, because He always lives to intercede for them.

In your own words, write what this Scripture means to you.

_____
_____
_____
_____
_____
_____

How can you apply this Scripture to your life today?

_____
_____
_____
_____
_____
_____

What have you prayed for and you received it immediately after you prayed?

_____
_____
_____
_____
_____
_____

Pray for 15 - 30 minutes and write any thoughts the Holy Spirit brings to your mind.

_____
_____
_____
_____
_____
_____
_____
_____

Today I will

_____
_____
_____
_____
_____
_____
_____
_____
_____
_____
_____
_____
_____

# DAY 19

Date_____

Psalm 34:17-18 (NIV)

The righteous cry out, and the Lord hears them; He delivers them from all their troubles. The Lord is close to the brokenhearted and saves those who are crushed in spirit.

In your own words, write what this Scripture means to you.

_____
_____
_____
_____
_____
_____

How can you apply this Scripture to your life today?

_____
_____
_____
_____
_____

What have you prayed for and you received it immediately after you prayed?

_____
_____
_____
_____
_____

Pray for 15 - 30 minutes and write any thoughts the Holy Spirit brings to your mind.

_____
_____
_____
_____
_____
_____
_____
_____

Today I will

_____
_____
_____
_____
_____
_____
_____
_____
_____
_____
_____
_____
_____
_____
_____

# DAY 20  Date_____

Romans 1:17 (NIV)

For in the gospel the righteousness of God is revealed—a righteousness that is by faith from first to last, just as it is written: "The righteous will live by faith."

In your own words, write what this Scripture means to you.

_____
_____
_____
_____
_____
_____

How can you apply this Scripture to your life today?

_____
_____
_____
_____
_____

What have you prayed for and you received it immediately after you prayed?

_____
_____
_____
_____
_____
_____

Pray for 15 - 30 minutes and write any thoughts the Holy Spirit brings to your mind.

_____
_____
_____
_____
_____
_____
_____

Today I will

---------------------------------------------------
---------------------------------------------------
---------------------------------------------------
---------------------------------------------------
---------------------------------------------------
---------------------------------------------------
---------------------------------------------------
_____
_____
_____
_____
_____
_____
_____

# DAY 21

Date_____

John 10:10 (NIV)
The thief comes only to steal and kill and destroy; I have come that they may have life, and have it to the full.

In your own words, write what this Scripture means to you.

_____
_____
_____
_____
_____
_____

How can you apply this Scripture to your life today?

_____
_____
_____
_____
_____
_____

What have you prayed for and you received it immediately after you prayed?

_____
_____
_____
_____
_____

Pray for 15 - 30 minutes and write any thoughts the Holy Spirit brings to your mind.

___

Today I will

# DAY 22

Date_____

1 Peter 3:21 (NIV)

And this water symbolizes baptism that now saves you also—not the removal of dirt from the body but the pledge of a clear conscience toward God. It saves you by the resurrection of Jesus Christ.

In your own words, write what this Scripture means to you.

_____
_____
_____
_____
_____
_____

How can you apply this Scripture to your life today?

_____
_____
_____
_____
_____
_____

What have you prayed for and you received it immediately after you prayed?

_____
_____
_____
_____
_____
_____

Pray for 15 - 30 minutes and write any thoughts the Holy Spirit brings to your mind.

Today I will

# DAY 23        Date_____

Psalm 103:12 (NIV)
As for as the east is from the west, so far has He removed our transgression from us.

In your own words, write what this Scripture means to you.
_____
_____
_____
_____
_____
_____

How can you apply this Scripture to your life today?
_____
_____
_____
_____
_____
_____

What have you prayed for and you received it immediately after you prayed?
_____
_____
_____
_____
_____
_____

Pray for 15 - 30 minutes and write any thoughts the Holy Spirit brings to your mind.

___

Today I will

___

# DAY 24

Date_____

Matthew 24:13 (NIV)
But the one who stands firm to the end will be saved.

In your own words, write what this Scripture means to you.

_____
_____
_____
_____
_____
_____

How can you apply this Scripture to your life today?

_____
_____
_____
_____
_____
_____

What have you prayed for and you received it immediately after you prayed?

_____
_____
_____
_____
_____
_____

Pray for 15 - 30 minutes and write any thoughts the Holy Spirit brings to your mind.

_____
_____
_____
_____
_____
_____
_____
_____

Today I will

_____
_____
_____
_____
_____
_____
_____
_____
_____
_____
_____
_____
_____
_____
_____

# DAY 25

Date_____

Isaiah 33:22 (NIV)
For the Lord is our judge, the Lord is our lawgiver; the Lord is our King; it is He who will save us.

In your own words, write what this Scripture means to you.

_____
_____
_____
_____
_____
_____

How can you apply this Scripture to your life today?

_____
_____
_____
_____
_____
_____

What have you prayed for and you received it immediately after you prayed?

_____
_____
_____
_____
_____
_____

Pray for 15 - 30 minutes and write any thoughts the Holy Spirit brings to your mind.

---

Today I will

# DAY 26

Date_____

Hebrews 5:9 (NIV)
And, once made perfect, He became the source of eternal salvation for all who obey Him.

In your own words, write what this Scripture means to you.

_____
_____
_____
_____
_____
_____

How can you apply this Scripture to your life today?

_____
_____
_____
_____
_____
_____

What have you prayed for and you received it immediately after you prayed?

_____
_____
_____
_____
_____
_____

Pray for 15 - 30 minutes and write any thoughts the Holy Spirit brings to your mind.

_____
_____
_____
_____
_____
_____
_____

Today I will

_____
_____
_____
_____
_____
_____
_____
_____
_____
_____
_____
_____
_____

# DAY 27

Date_____

I Peter 2:2 (NIV)
Like newborn babies, crave pure spiritual milk, so that by it you may grow up in your salvation.

In your own words, write what this Scripture means to you.

_____
_____
_____
_____
_____
_____

How can you apply this Scripture to your life today?

_____
_____
_____
_____
_____
_____

What have you prayed for and you received it immediately after you prayed?

_____
_____
_____
_____
_____
_____

Pray for 15 - 30 minutes and write any thoughts the Holy Spirit brings to your mind.

___

Today I will

___

# DAY 28

Date_____

Mark 8:35 (NIV)

For whoever wants to save their life will lose it, but whoever loses their life for Me and for the gospel will save it.

In your own words, write what this Scripture means to you.

_____
_____
_____
_____
_____
_____

How can you apply this Scripture to your life today?

_____
_____
_____
_____
_____
_____

What have you prayed for and you received it immediately after you prayed?

_____
_____
_____
_____
_____
_____

Pray for 15 - 30 minutes and write any thoughts the Holy Spirit brings to your mind.

___

Today I will

___

# DAY 29

Date_____

Ezekiel 36:26 (NIV)

I will give you a new heart and put a new spirit in you; I will remove from you your heart of stone and give you a heart of flesh.

In your own words, write what this Scripture means to you.

_____
_____
_____
_____
_____
_____

How can you apply this Scripture to your life today?

_____
_____
_____
_____
_____

What have you prayed for and you received it immediately after you prayed?

_____
_____
_____
_____
_____
_____

Pray for 15 - 30 minutes and write any thoughts the Holy Spirit brings to your mind.

_____
_____
_____
_____
_____
_____
_____

Today I will

_____
_____
_____
_____
_____
_____
_____
_____
_____
_____
_____
_____
_____
_____

# DAY 30

Date_____

Isaiah 44:22 (NIV)
I have swept away your offenses like a cloud, your sins like the morning mist. Return to Me, for I have redeemed you.

In your own words, write what this Scripture means to you.

_____
_____
_____
_____
_____
_____

How can you apply this Scripture to your life today?

_____
_____
_____
_____
_____
_____

What have you prayed for and you received it immediately after you prayed?

_____
_____
_____
_____
_____
_____

Pray for 15 - 30 minutes and write any thoughts the Holy Spirit brings to your mind.

___

Today I will

___

# MAY

## *Faith*

THE WALK OF FAITH JOURNALS
*Building Your Faith Daily*

Book 5

Brenda Williams

# MAY

Book 5 in The Walk of Faith Journals

## Faith

This Journal will give you a Scripture every day to read, meditate, and memorize. Read the Scripture three times a day. Ask the Holy Spirit to help you memorize the Scripture and give you revelation on His Word.

## REFLECTION

I believe because there is a knowing anchored in the fact that You love me with an everlasting love. I can have faith based on that alone. You are a good, loving Father who cares about every aspect of my life. My faith hinges on that. Therefore, I can have faith for healing, faith for deliverance, faith for prosperity, and faith for answered prayer. I know that You will and can never fail me. That is not who You are. The essence of Your being is love. That is the God who hastens His Word to perform it in MY LIFE. Having faith in You, my God, should never be optional, but a given!

# DAY 1

Date_____

Hebrews 11:1 (ESV)
Now faith is the assurance of things hoped for, the conviction of things not seen.

In your own words, write what this Scripture means to you.

_____
_____
_____
_____
_____
_____

How can you apply this Scripture to your life today?

_____
_____
_____
_____
_____
_____

What have you prayed for and you received it immediately after you prayed?

_____
_____
_____
_____
_____
_____

Pray for 15 - 30 minutes and write any thoughts the Holy Spirit brings to your mind.

_____

_____

_____

_____

_____

_____

_____

Today I will

_____

_____

_____

_____

_____

_____

_____

_____

_____

_____

_____

_____

# DAY 2

Date_____

Proverbs 3:5-6 (ESV)

Trust in the Lord with all your heart, and do not lean on your own understanding. In all your ways acknowledge Him, and He will make straight your paths.

In your own words, write what this Scripture means to you.

_____
_____
_____
_____
_____
_____

How can you apply this Scripture to your life today?

_____
_____
_____
_____
_____
_____

What have you prayed for and you received it immediately after you prayed?

-----------------------------------------------
-----------------------------------------------
-----------------------------------------------
-----------------------------------------------
-----------------------------------------------
-----------------------------------------------

Pray for 15 - 30 minutes and write any thoughts the Holy Spirit brings to your mind.

_____
_____
_____
_____
_____
_____
_____
_____

Today I will

_____
_____
_____
_____
_____
_____
_____
_____
_____
_____
_____
_____
_____
_____
_____

# DAY 3                        Date_____

John 10:10 (ESV)
The thief comes only to steal and kill and destroy. I came that they may have life and have it abundantly.

In your own words, write what this Scripture means to you.
_____
_____
_____
_____
_____
_____

How can you apply this Scripture to your life today?
_____
_____
_____
_____
_____
_____

What have you prayed for and you received it immediately after you prayed?
_____
_____
_____
_____
_____
_____

Pray for 15 - 30 minutes and write any thoughts the Holy Spirit brings to your mind.

___

Today I will
___

# DAY 4

Date_____

Colossians 1:13 (ESV)
He has delivered us from the dominion of darkness and transferred us to the kingdom of His beloved Son.

In your own words, write what this Scripture means to you.

_____
_____
_____
_____
_____

How can you apply this Scripture to your life today?

_____
_____
_____
_____
_____

What have you prayed for and you received it immediately after you prayed?

_____
_____
_____
_____
_____

Pray for 15 - 30 minutes and write any thoughts the Holy Spirit brings to your mind.

Today I will

# DAY 5

Date_____

2 Corinthians 5:17 (ESV)
Therefore, if anyone is in Christ, he is a new creation. The old has passed away; behold, the new has come.

In your own words, write what this Scripture means to you.

_____
_____
_____
_____
_____
_____

How can you apply this Scripture to your life today?

_____
_____
_____
_____
_____

What have you prayed for and you received it immediately after you prayed?

_____
_____
_____
_____
_____
_____

Pray for 15 - 30 minutes and write any thoughts the Holy Spirit brings to your mind.

Today I will

# DAY 6

Date_____

John 15:7 (ESV)
If you abide in Me, and My Words abide in you, ask whatever you wish, and it will be done for you.

In your own words, write what this Scripture means to you.
_____
_____
_____
_____
_____
_____

How can you apply this Scripture to your life today?
_____
_____
_____
_____
_____
_____

What have you prayed for and you received it immediately after you prayed?
_____
_____
_____
_____
_____
_____

Pray for 15 - 30 minutes and write any thoughts the Holy Spirit brings to your mind.

_____
_____
_____
_____
_____
_____
_____

Today I will

_____
_____
_____
_____
_____
_____
_____
_____
_____
_____
_____
_____
_____
_____

# DAY 7                    Date_____

Isaiah 41:10 (ESV)

Fear not, for I am with you; be not dismayed, for I am your God; I will strengthen you, I will help you, I will uphold you with My righteous right hand,

In your own words, write what this Scripture means to you.

_____
_____
_____
_____
_____
_____

How can you apply this Scripture to your life today?

_____
_____
_____
_____
_____

What have you prayed for and you received it immediately after you prayed?

_____
_____
_____
_____
_____
_____

Pray for 15 - 30 minutes and write any thoughts the Holy Spirit brings to your mind.

_____
_____
_____
_____
_____
_____
_____

Today I will

_____
_____
_____
_____
_____
_____
_____
_____
_____
_____
_____
_____
_____
_____

# DAY 8                    Date_____

Matthew 17:20 (ESV)

He said to them, "Because of your little faith. For truly, I say to you, if you have faith like a grain of mustard seed, you will say to this mountain, 'Move from here to there,' and it will move, and nothing will be impossible for you."

In your own words, write what this Scripture means to you.

_____
_____
_____
_____
_____
_____
_____

How can you apply this Scripture to your life today?

_____
_____
_____
_____
_____
_____

What have you prayed for and you received it immediately after you prayed?

_____
_____
_____
_____
_____

Pray for 15 - 30 minutes and write any thoughts the Holy Spirit brings to your mind.

Today I will

# DAY 9                    Date_____

2 Timothy 1:7 (ESV)
For God gave us a spirit not of fear but of power and love and self-control.

In your own words, write what this Scripture means to you.

_____
_____
_____
_____
_____
_____

How can you apply this Scripture to your life today?

_____
_____
_____
_____
_____
_____

What have you prayed for and you received it immediately after you prayed?

_____
_____
_____
_____
_____
_____

Pray for 15 - 30 minutes and write any thoughts the Holy Spirit brings to your mind.

---

Today I will

# DAY 10

Date_____

Romans 10:9-10 (ESV)

Because, if you confess with your mouth that Jesus is Lord and believe in your heart that God raised Him from the dead, you will be saved. For with the heart one believes and is justified, and with the mouth one confesses and is saved.

In your own words, write what this Scripture means to you.

_____
_____
_____
_____
_____
_____

How can you apply this Scripture to your life today?

_____
_____
_____
_____
_____

What have you prayed for and you received it immediately after you prayed?

_____
_____
_____
_____
_____

Pray for 15 - 30 minutes and write any thoughts the Holy Spirit brings to your mind.

Today I will

# DAY 11

Date_____

Romans 8:28 (ESV)
And we know that for those who love God all things work together for good, for those who are called according to His purpose.

In your own words, write what this Scripture means to you.

_____
_____
_____
_____
_____


How can you apply this Scripture to your life today?

_____
_____
_____
_____
_____


What have you prayed for and you received it immediately after you prayed?

_____
_____
_____
_____
_____

Pray for 15 - 30 minutes and write any thoughts the Holy Spirit brings to your mind.

_____

_____

_____

_____

_____

_____

_____

Today I will

_____

_____

_____

_____

_____

_____

_____

_____

_____

_____

_____

_____

_____

_____

_____

# DAY 12

Date_____

Matthew 7:7-8 (ESV)

Ask, and it will be given to you, seek, and you will find, knock, and it will be opened to you. For everyone who asks receives, and the one who seeks find, and to the one who knocks it will be opened.

In your own words, write what this Scripture means to you.

_____
_____
_____
_____
_____
_____

How can you apply this Scripture to your life today?

_____
_____
_____
_____
_____
_____

What have you prayed for and you received it immediately after you prayed?

_____
_____
_____
_____
_____

Pray for 15 - 30 minutes and write any thoughts the Holy Spirit brings to your mind.

___

Today I will

# DAY 13

Date_____

Deuteronomy 31:6 (ESV)

Be strong and courageous. Do not fear or be in dread of them, for it is the Lord your God who goes with you. He will not leave you or forsake you.

In your own words, write what this Scripture means to you.

_____
_____
_____
_____
_____
_____

How can you apply this Scripture to your life today?

_____
_____
_____
_____
_____

What have you prayed for and you received it immediately after you prayed?

_____
_____
_____
_____
_____
_____

Pray for 15 - 30 minutes and write any thoughts the Holy Spirit brings to your mind.

_____
_____
_____
_____
_____
_____
_____
_____

Today I will

_____
_____
_____
_____
_____
_____
_____
_____
_____
_____
_____
_____
_____
_____
_____

# DAY 14

Date_____

Philippians 4:13 (ESV)

I can do all things through Him who strengthens me.

In your own words, write what this Scripture means to you.

_____
_____
_____
_____
_____
_____
_____

How can you apply this Scripture to your life today?

_____
_____
_____
_____
_____
_____
_____

What have you prayed for and you received it immediately after you prayed?

_____
_____
_____
_____
_____
_____

Pray for 15 - 30 minutes and write any thoughts the Holy Spirit brings to your mind.

Today I will

# DAY 15

Date_____

Ephesians 2:8 (ESV)
For by grace you have been saved through faith. And this is not your own doing; it is the gift of God.

In your own words, write what this Scripture means to you.

_____
_____
_____
_____
_____
_____

How can you apply this Scripture to your life today?

_____
_____
_____
_____
_____
_____

What have you prayed for and you received it immediately after you prayed?

_____
_____
_____
_____
_____
_____

Pray for 15 - 30 minutes and write any thoughts the Holy Spirit brings to your mind.

_____
_____
_____
_____
_____
_____
_____

Today I will

_____
_____
_____
_____
_____
_____
_____
_____
_____
_____
_____
_____
_____

# DAY 16

Date_____

John 16:33 (ESV)

I have said these things to you, that in Me you may have peace. In the world you will have tribulation. But take heart; I have overcome the world.

In your own words, write what this Scripture means to you.

_____
_____
_____
_____
_____
_____

How can you apply this Scripture to your life today?

_____
_____
_____
_____
_____

What have you prayed for and you received it immediately after you prayed?

_____
_____
_____
_____
_____
_____

Pray for 15 - 30 minutes and write any thoughts the Holy Spirit brings to your mind.

_____
_____
_____
_____
_____
_____
_____

Today I will

_____
_____
_____
_____
_____
_____
_____
_____
_____
_____
_____
_____
_____

# DAY 17                    Date_____

John 3:16 (ESV)
For God so loved the world, that He gave His only Son, that whoever believes in Him should not perish but have eternal life.

In your own words, write what this Scripture means to you.

_____
_____
_____
_____
_____
_____


How can you apply this Scripture to your life today?

_____
_____
_____
_____
_____
_____


What have you prayed for and you received it immediately after you prayed?

_____
_____
_____
_____
_____
_____

Pray for 15 - 30 minutes and write any thoughts the Holy Spirit brings to your mind.

_____
_____
_____
_____
_____
_____
_____

Today I will

_____
_____
_____
_____
_____
_____
_____
_____
_____
_____
_____
_____
_____
_____
_____

# **DAY 18**                    Date_____

1 Peter 5:7 (ESV)
Casting all your anxieties on Him, because He cares for you.

In your own words, write what this Scripture means to you.
_____
_____
_____
_____
_____
_____

How can you apply this Scripture to your life today?
_____
_____
_____
_____
_____

What have you prayed for and you received it immediately after you prayed?
_____
_____
_____
_____
_____
_____

Pray for 15 - 30 minutes and write any thoughts the Holy Spirit brings to your mind.

Today I will

# DAY 19

Date_____

James 1:2-4 (ESV)

Count it all joy, my brothers, when you meet trials of various kinds, for you know that testing of your faith produces steadfastness. And let Steadfastness have its full effect, that you may be perfect and complete, lacking nothing.

In your own words, write what this Scripture means to you.

_____
_____
_____
_____
_____
_____

How can you apply this Scripture to your life today?

_____
_____
_____
_____
_____

What have you prayed for and you received it immediately after you prayed?

-----------------------------------------------------------------
-----------------------------------------------------------------
-----------------------------------------------------------------
-----------------------------------------------------------------
-----------------------------------------------------------------

Pray for 15 - 30 minutes and write any thoughts the Holy Spirit brings to your mind.

___

Today I will

___

# DAY 20

Date_____

Hebrews 13:5 (ESV)

Keep your life free from love of money, and be content with what you have, for He has said, "I will never leave you nor forsake you."

In your own words, write what this Scripture means to you.

_____
_____
_____
_____
_____
_____

How can you apply this Scripture to your life today?

_____
_____
_____
_____
_____
_____

What have you prayed for and you received it immediately after you prayed?

_____
_____
_____
_____
_____
_____

Pray for 15 - 30 minutes and write any thoughts the Holy Spirit brings to your mind.

_____
_____
_____
_____
_____
_____
_____

Today I will

_____
_____
_____
_____
_____
_____
_____
_____
_____
_____
_____
_____
_____
_____

# DAY 21

Date_____

Ephesians 2:8-9 (ESV)

For by grace you have been saved through faith. And this is not your own doing; it is the gift of God, not a result of works, so that no one may boast.

In your own words, write what this Scripture means to you.

_____
_____
_____
_____
_____
_____

How can you apply this Scripture to your life today?

_____
_____
_____
_____
_____
_____

What have you prayed for and you received it immediately after you prayed?

_____
_____
_____
_____
_____
_____

Pray for 15 - 30 minutes and write any thoughts the Holy Spirit brings to your mind.

___

Today I will

# DAY 22

Date_____

2 Corinthians 5:7 (ESV)

For we walk by faith, not by sight.

In your own words, write what this Scripture means to you.

_____
_____
_____
_____
_____

How can you apply this Scripture to your life today?

_____
_____
_____
_____
_____

What have you prayed for and you received it immediately after you prayed?

_____
_____
_____
_____
_____
_____

Pray for 15 - 30 minutes and write any thoughts the Holy Spirit brings to your mind.

___

Today I will

___

# DAY 23

Date_____

Ephesians 6:16 (ESV)

In all circumstances take up the shield of faith with which you can extinguish all the flaming darts of the evil one.

In your own words, write what this Scripture means to you.

_____
_____
_____
_____
_____
_____

How can you apply this Scripture to your life today?

_____
_____
_____
_____
_____

What have you prayed for and you received it immediately after you prayed?

_____
_____
_____
_____
_____
_____

Pray for 15 - 30 minutes and write any thoughts the Holy Spirit brings to your mind.

___

Today I will

___

# DAY 24

Date_____

1 Corinthians 3:11 (ESV)

For no one can lay a foundation other than that which is laid, which is Jesus Christ.

In your own words, write what this Scripture means to you.

_____
_____
_____
_____
_____
_____

How can you apply this Scripture to your life today?

_____
_____
_____
_____
_____
_____

What have you prayed for and you received it immediately after you prayed?

_____
_____
_____
_____
_____
_____

Pray for 15 - 30 minutes and write any thoughts the Holy Spirit brings to your mind.

_____
_____
_____
_____
_____
_____
_____

Today I will

_____
_____
_____
_____
_____
_____
_____
_____
_____
_____
_____
_____
_____
_____
_____

# DAY 25

Date_____

Romans 8:37 (ESV)
No, in all these things we are more than conquerors through Him who loves us.

In your own words, write what this Scripture means to you.

_____
_____
_____
_____
_____
_____

How can you apply this Scripture to your life today?

_____
_____
_____
_____
_____
_____

What have you prayed for and you received it immediately after you prayed?

------------------------------
------------------------------
------------------------------
------------------------------
------------------------------
------------------------------

Pray for 15 - 30 minutes and write any thoughts the Holy Spirit brings to your mind.

_____
_____
_____
_____
_____
_____
_____
_____

Today I will

_____
_____
_____
_____
_____
_____
_____
_____
_____
_____
_____
_____
_____
_____

# DAY 26

Date_____

Romans 1:17 (ESV)

For in it the righteousness of God is revealed from faith for faith, as it is written, "The righteous shall live by faith."

In your own words, write what this Scripture means to you.

_____
_____
_____
_____
_____
_____

How can you apply this Scripture to your life today?

_____
_____
_____
_____
_____

What have you prayed for and you received it immediately after you prayed?

_____
_____
_____
_____
_____
_____

Pray for 15 - 30 minutes and write any thoughts the Holy Spirit brings to your mind.

Today I will

# DAY 27

Date_____

John 14:14 (ESV)
If you ask Me anything in My name, I will do it.

In your own words, write what this Scripture means to you.
_____
_____
_____
_____
_____
_____

How can you apply this Scripture to your life today?
_____
_____
_____
_____
_____

What have you prayed for and you received it immediately after you prayed?
_____
_____
_____
_____
_____
_____

Pray for 15 - 30 minutes and write any thoughts the Holy Spirit brings to your mind.

---

Today I will

# DAY 28

Date_____

Isaiah 40:31 (ESV)

But they who wait for the Lord shall renew their strength; they shall mount up with wings like eagles; they shall run and not be weary; they shall walk and not faint.

In your own words, write what this Scripture means to you.

_____
_____
_____
_____
_____
_____

How can you apply this Scripture to your life today?

_____
_____
_____
_____
_____
_____

What have you prayed for and you received it immediately after you prayed?

_____
_____
_____
_____
_____
_____

Pray for 15 - 30 minutes and write any thoughts the Holy Spirit brings to your mind.

_____
_____
_____
_____
_____
_____
_____
_____

Today I will

_____
_____
_____
_____
_____
_____
_____
_____
_____
_____
_____
_____
_____
_____

# DAY 29

Date_____

1 John 5:4 (ESV)

For everyone who has been born of God overcomes the world. And this is the victory that has overcome the world— our faith.

In your own words, write what this Scripture means to you.

_____
_____
_____
_____
_____
_____

How can you apply this Scripture to your life today?

_____
_____
_____
_____
_____

What have you prayed for and you received it immediately after you prayed?

_____
_____
_____
_____
_____
_____

Pray for 15 - 30 minutes and write any thoughts the Holy Spirit brings to your mind.

___

Today I will

# DAY 30

Date_____

Hebrews 11:3 (ESV)

By faith we understand that the universe was created by the Word of God, so that what is seen was not made out of things that are visible.

In your own words, write what this Scripture means to you.

_____
_____
_____
_____
_____
_____

How can you apply this Scripture to your life today?

_____
_____
_____
_____
_____

What have you prayed for and you received it immediately after you prayed?

_____
_____
_____
_____
_____
_____

Pray for 15 - 30 minutes and write any thoughts the Holy Spirit brings to your mind.

___

Today I will

___

# DAY 31

Date_____

Ephesians 2:8 (ESV)

For by grace you have been saved through faith. And this is not your own doing; it is the gift of God.

In your own words, write what this Scripture means to you.

_____
_____
_____
_____
_____
_____

How can you apply this Scripture to your life today?

_____
_____
_____
_____
_____
_____

What have you prayed for and you received it immediately after you prayed?

_____
_____
_____
_____
_____
_____

Pray for 15 - 30 minutes and write any thoughts the Holy Spirit brings to your mind.

___

Today I will

___

# JUNE

## *Grace*

### THE WALK OF FAITH JOURNALS
*Building Your Faith Daily*

Book 6

Brenda Williams

## JUNE

Book 6 in The Walk of Faith Journals

## Grace

This Journal will give you a Scripture every day to read, meditate, and memorize.  Read the Scripture three times a day  Ask the Holy Spirit to help you memorize the Scripture and give you revelation on His Word.

## Reflection

## *Grace*

Your mercy really does endure forever. You have not allowed me to be consumed by evil. You continually appropriate the grace that causes me to triumph. I experience one victory after another. With each, I am empowered because of Your grace. So often I did not get what I deserved and got what I never expected or should have received. Your mercies are new daily. With whatever challenges and obstacles I may find, Your mercies and grace meet me at the point of intersection, allowing and enabling me to move forward in victory.

# DAY 1                                   Date_____

Hebrews 4:16 (KJV)
Let us come boldly unto the throne of grace, that we may obtain Mercy, and find peace to help in time of need.

In your own words, write what this Scripture means to you.
_____
_____
_____
_____
_____
_____

How can you apply this Scripture to your life today?
_____
_____
_____
_____
_____
_____

What have you prayed for and you received it immediately after you prayed?
_____
_____
_____
_____
_____
_____

Pray for 15 - 30 minutes and write any thoughts the Holy Spirit brings to your mind.

___

Today I will

___

# DAY 2    Date_____

Ephesians 2: 4-5 (KJV)

But God, who is rich in Mercy, for His great love wherewith He loved us, Even when we were dead in sins, hath quickened us together with Christ, (by grace ye are saved).

In your own words, write what this Scripture means to you.

_____
_____
_____
_____
_____
_____

How can you apply this Scripture to your life today?

_____
_____
_____
_____
_____
_____

What have you prayed for and you received it immediately after you prayed?

-----------------------------------------------
-----------------------------------------------
-----------------------------------------------
-----------------------------------------------
-----------------------------------------------
-----------------------------------------------

Pray for 15 - 30 minutes and write any thoughts the Holy Spirit brings to your mind.

---

Today I will

# DAY 3                    Date_____

Psalm 103:8 (KJV)
The Lord is merciful and gracious, slow to anger, and plenteous in Mercy.

In your own words, write what this Scripture means to you.

_____
_____
_____
_____
_____
_____

How can you apply this Scripture to your life today?

_____
_____
_____
_____
_____

What have you prayed for and you received it immediately after you prayed?

_____
_____
_____
_____
_____
_____

Pray for 15 - 30 minutes and write any thoughts the Holy Spirit brings to your mind.

___

Today I will

___

# DAY 4	Date_____

Psalm 103:8 (KJV)
The Lord is merciful and gracious, slow to anger, and plenteous in Mercy.

In your own words, write what this Scripture means to you.
_____
_____
_____
_____
_____
_____

How can you apply this Scripture to your life today?
_____
_____
_____
_____
_____
_____

What have you prayed for and you received it immediately after you prayed?
_____
_____
_____
_____
_____
_____

Pray for 15 - 30 minutes and write any thoughts the Holy Spirit brings to your mind.

_____
_____
_____
_____
_____
_____
_____

Today I will

_____
_____
_____
_____
_____
_____
_____
_____
_____
_____
_____

# DAY 5

Date_____

1 Peter 5:10 (KJV)

But the God of all grace, who hath called us unto His eternal glory by Christ Jesus, after that ye have suffered a while, make you perfect, stablish, strengthen, settle you!

In your own words, write what this Scripture means to you.

_____
_____
_____
_____
_____
_____
_____

How can you apply this Scripture to your life today?

_____
_____
_____
_____
_____
_____

What have you prayed for and you received it immediately after you prayed?

_____
_____
_____
_____
_____
_____

Pray for 15 - 30 minutes and write any thoughts the Holy Spirit brings to your mind.

_____
_____
_____
_____
_____
_____
_____
_____

Today I will

_____
_____
_____
_____
_____
_____
_____
_____
_____
_____
_____
_____
_____
_____
_____
_____

# DAY 6

Date_____

Titus 2:11-12 (KJV)

For the grace of God that bringeth salvation hath appeared to all men, Teaching us that, denying ungodliness and worldly lusts, we should live soberly, righteously, and godly, in this present world.

In your own words, write what this Scripture means to you.

_____
_____
_____
_____
_____
_____

How can you apply this Scripture to your life today?

_____
_____
_____
_____
_____

What have you prayed for and you received it immediately after you prayed?

_____
_____
_____
_____
_____
_____

Pray for 15 - 30 minutes and write any thoughts the Holy Spirit brings to your mind.

_____
_____
_____
_____
_____
_____
_____

Today I will

_____
_____
_____
_____
_____
_____
_____
_____
_____
_____
_____
_____
_____

# DAY 7

Date_____

Matthew 6:14 (KJV)

For if ye forgive men their trespasses, your heavenly Father will also forgive you.

In your own words, write what this Scripture means to you.

_____
_____
_____
_____
_____
_____

How can you apply this Scripture to your life today?

_____
_____
_____
_____
_____
_____

What have you prayed for and you received it immediately after you prayed?

_____
_____
_____
_____
_____
_____

Pray for 15 - 30 minutes and write any thoughts the Holy Spirit brings to your mind.

---

Today I will

# DAY 8

Date_____

2 Timothy 1:9 (KJV)

Who hath saved us, and called us with an holy calling, not according to our works, but according to His own purpose and grace, which was given us in Christ Jesus before the world began.

In your own words, write what this Scripture means to you.

_____
_____
_____
_____
_____
_____

How can you apply this Scripture to your life today?

_____
_____
_____
_____
_____

What have you prayed for and you received it immediately after you prayed?

_____
_____
_____
_____
_____
_____

Pray for 15 - 30 minutes and write any thoughts the Holy Spirit brings to your mind.

_____
_____
_____
_____
_____
_____
_____

Today I will

_____
_____
_____
_____
_____
_____
_____
_____
_____
_____
_____
_____
_____
_____
_____

# DAY 9

Date_____

Romans 6:14 (KJV)

For sin shall not have dominion over you: for ye are not under the law, but under grace.

In your own words, write what this Scripture means to you.

_____
_____
_____
_____
_____
_____

How can you apply this Scripture to your life today?

_____
_____
_____
_____
_____
_____

What have you prayed for and you received it immediately after you prayed?

------------------------------------------------------------
------------------------------------------------------------
------------------------------------------------------------
------------------------------------------------------------
------------------------------------------------------------
------------------------------------------------------------

Pray for 15 - 30 minutes and write any thoughts the Holy Spirit brings to your mind.

_____
_____
_____
_____
_____
_____
_____

Today I will

_____
_____
_____
_____
_____
_____
_____
_____
_____
_____
_____
_____
_____
_____

# DAY 10

Date_____

Revelation 22:21 (KJV)

The grace of our Lord Jesus Christ be with you all. Amen.

In your own words, write what this Scripture means to you.

_____
_____
_____
_____
_____
_____

How can you apply this Scripture to your life today?

_____
_____
_____
_____
_____
_____

What have you prayed for and you received it immediately after you prayed?

_____
_____
_____
_____
_____
_____

Pray for 15 - 30 minutes and write any thoughts the Holy Spirit brings to your mind.

_____
_____
_____
_____
_____
_____
_____

Today I will

_____
_____
_____
_____
_____
_____
_____
_____
_____
_____
_____
_____
_____

# DAY 11

Date_____

Romans 3:23-24 (KJV)

For all have sinned, and come short of the glory of God; Being justified freely by His grace through the redemption that is in Christ Jesus.

In your own words, write what this Scripture means to you.

_____
_____
_____
_____
_____
_____

How can you apply this Scripture to your life today?

_____
_____
_____
_____
_____

What have you prayed for and you received it immediately after you prayed?

_____
_____
_____
_____
_____
_____

Pray for 15 - 30 minutes and write any thoughts the Holy Spirit brings to your mind.

---

Today I will

# DAY 12

Date_____

Romans 6:15 (KJV)

What then? Shall we sin, because we are not under the law, but under grace? God forbid.

In your own words, write what this Scripture means to you.

_____
_____
_____
_____
_____
_____

How can you apply this Scripture to your life today?

_____
_____
_____
_____
_____
_____

What have you prayed for and you received it immediately after you prayed?

_____
_____
_____
_____
_____
_____

Pray for 15 - 30 minutes and write any thoughts the Holy Spirit brings to your mind.

_____
_____
_____
_____
_____
_____
_____

Today I will

_____
_____
_____
_____
_____
_____
_____
_____
_____
_____
_____
_____
_____
_____

# DAY 13          Date_____

Psalm 90:17 (KJV)
And let the beauty of the Lord our God be upon us: and establish thou the work of our hands upon us; yea, the work of our hands establish thou it.

In your own words, write what this Scripture means to you.

_____
_____
_____
_____
_____
_____
_____

How can you apply this Scripture to your life today?

_____
_____
_____
_____
_____
_____

What have you prayed for and you received it immediately after you prayed?

_____
_____
_____
_____
_____
_____

Pray for 15 - 30 minutes and write any thoughts the Holy Spirit brings to your mind.

_____
_____
_____
_____
_____
_____
_____

Today I will

_____
_____
_____
_____
_____
_____
_____
_____
_____
_____
_____

# DAY 14                    Date_____

John 3:16 (KJV)

For God so loved the world, that He gave His only begotten Son, that whosoever believeth in Him should not perish, but have everlasting life.

In your own words, write what this Scripture means to you.

_____
_____
_____
_____
_____
_____
_____

How can you apply this Scripture to your life today?

_____
_____
_____
_____
_____
_____
_____

What have you prayed for and you received it immediately after you prayed?

_____
_____
_____
_____
_____
_____

Pray for 15 - 30 minutes and write any thoughts the Holy Spirit brings to your mind.

_____
_____
_____
_____
_____
_____
_____

Today I will

_____
_____
_____
_____
_____
_____
_____
_____
_____
_____
_____
_____

# DAY 15

Date_____

Ephesians 2:8-9 (KJV)

For by grace are ye saved through faith; and that not of yourselves; it is the gift of God: Not of works, lest any man should boast.

In your own words, write what this Scripture means to you.

_____
_____
_____
_____
_____
_____

How can you apply this Scripture to your life today?

_____
_____
_____
_____
_____

What have you prayed for and you received it immediately after you prayed?

_____
_____
_____
_____
_____
_____

Pray for 15 - 30 minutes and write any thoughts the Holy Spirit brings to your mind.

_____
_____
_____
_____
_____
_____
_____

Today I will

_____
_____
_____
_____
_____
_____
_____
_____
_____
_____
_____
_____
_____
_____

# DAY 16

Date_____

2 Chronicles 30:9b (KJV)

For the Lord your God is gracious and merciful, and will not turn away His face from you, if ye return unto Him.

In your own words, write what this Scripture means to you.

_____
_____
_____
_____
_____
_____

How can you apply this Scripture to your life today?

_____
_____
_____
_____
_____
_____

What have you prayed for and you received it immediately after you prayed?

_____
_____
_____
_____
_____
_____

Pray for 15 - 30 minutes and write any thoughts the Holy Spirit brings to your mind.

---
---
---
---
---
---
---

Today I will

---
---
---
---
---
---
---
---
---
---
---
---
---

# DAY 17                    Date_____

Psalm 23:6 (KJV)

Surely goodness and mercy shall follow me all the days of my life: and I will dwell in the house of the Lord forever.

In your own words, write what this Scripture means to you.

_____
_____
_____
_____
_____
_____

How can you apply this Scripture to your life today?

_____
_____
_____
_____
_____
_____

What have you prayed for and you received it immediately after you prayed?

_____
_____
_____
_____
_____
_____

Pray for 15 - 30 minutes and write any thoughts the Holy Spirit brings to your mind.

Today I will

# DAY 18

Date_____

1 Peter 1:13 (KJV)

Wherefore gird up the loins of your mind, be sober, and hope to the end for the grace that is to be brought unto you at the revelation of Jesus Christ.

In your own words, write what this Scripture means to you.

_____
_____
_____
_____
_____
_____

How can you apply this Scripture to your life today?

_____
_____
_____
_____
_____
_____

What have you prayed for and you received it immediately after you prayed?

_____
_____
_____
_____
_____
_____

Pray for 15 - 30 minutes and write any thoughts the Holy Spirit brings to your mind.

_____
_____
_____
_____
_____
_____
_____

Today I will

_____
_____
_____
_____
_____
_____
_____
_____
_____
_____
_____
_____

# DAY 19                    Date_____

2 Corinthians 12:9 (KJV)

And He said unto me, My grace is sufficient for thee; for My strength is made perfect in weakness. Most gladly therefore will I rather glory in my infirmities, that the power of Christ may rest upon me.

In your own words, write what this Scripture means to you.

_____
_____
_____
_____
_____
_____

How can you apply this Scripture to your life today?

_____
_____
_____
_____
_____
_____

What have you prayed for and you received it immediately after you prayed?

_____
_____
_____
_____
_____

Pray for 15 - 30 minutes and write any thoughts the Holy Spirit brings to your mind.

___

Today I will

___

# DAY 20    Date_____

2 Peter 3:18 (KJV)

But grow in grace, and in the knowledge of our Lord and Saviour Jesus Christ. To Him be glory both now and forever. Amen.

In your own words, write what this Scripture means to you.

_____
_____
_____
_____
_____
_____

How can you apply this Scripture to your life today?

_____
_____
_____
_____
_____

What have you prayed for and you received it immediately after you prayed?

_____
_____
_____
_____
_____
_____

Pray for 15 - 30 minutes and write any thoughts the Holy Spirit brings to your mind.

_____
_____
_____
_____
_____
_____
_____

Today I will

_____
_____
_____
_____
_____
_____
_____
_____
_____
_____
_____
_____

# DAY 21

Date_____

Romans 12:3 (KJV)

For I say, through the grace given unto me, to every man that is among you, not to think of himself more highly than he ought to think; but think soberly, according as God hath dealt to every man the measure of faith.

In your own words, write what this Scripture means to you.

_____
_____
_____
_____
_____
_____
_____

How can you apply this Scripture to your life today?

_____
_____
_____
_____
_____

What have you prayed for and you received it immediately after you prayed?

_____
_____
_____
_____
_____

Pray for 15 - 30 minutes and write any thoughts the Holy Spirit brings to your mind.

___

Today I will

___

# DAY 22

Date_____

Nehemiah 9:31 (KJV)

Nevertheless for thy great mercies' sake thou didst not utterly consume them, nor forsake them; for thou art a gracious and merciful God.

In your own words, write what this Scripture means to you.

_____
_____
_____
_____
_____
_____
_____

How can you apply this Scripture to your life today?

_____
_____
_____
_____
_____
_____

What have you prayed for and you received it immediately after you prayed?

_____
_____
_____
_____
_____
_____

Pray for 15 - 30 minutes and write any thoughts the Holy Spirit brings to your mind.

Today I will

# DAY 23

Date_____

2 Corinthians 13:14 (KJV)
The grace of the Lord Jesus Christ, and the love of God, and the communion of the Holy Ghost, be with you all. Amen.

In your own words, write what this Scripture means to you.

_____
_____
_____
_____
_____
_____

How can you apply this Scripture to your life today?

_____
_____
_____
_____
_____
_____

What have you prayed for and you received it immediately after you prayed?

_____
_____
_____
_____
_____
_____

Pray for 15 - 30 minutes and write any thoughts the Holy Spirit brings to your mind.

_____
_____
_____
_____
_____
_____
_____

Today I will

_____
_____
_____
_____
_____
_____
_____
_____
_____
_____
_____
_____
_____

# DAY 24          Date_____

Numbers 6:24-26 (KJV)

The Lord bless thee, and keep thee: The Lord make His face shine upon thee, and be gracious unto thee: The Lord lift up His countenance upon thee, and give thee peace.

In your own words, write what this Scripture means to you.

_____
_____
_____
_____
_____
_____

How can you apply this Scripture to your life today?

_____
_____
_____
_____
_____
_____

What have you prayed for and you received it immediately after you prayed?

_____
_____
_____
_____
_____
_____

Pray for 15 - 30 minutes and write any thoughts the Holy Spirit brings to your mind.

_____
_____
_____
_____
_____
_____
_____
_____

Today I will

_____
_____
_____
_____
_____
_____
_____
_____
_____
_____
_____
_____
_____

# DAY 25

Date_____

Romans 5:21 (KJV)
That as sin hath reigned unto death even so might grace reign through righteousness unto eternal life by Jesus Christ our Lord.

In your own words, write what this Scripture means to you.

_____
_____
_____
_____
_____
_____

How can you apply this Scripture to your life today?

_____
_____
_____
_____
_____

What have you prayed for and you received it immediately after you prayed?

_____
_____
_____
_____
_____

Pray for 15 - 30 minutes and write any thoughts the Holy Spirit brings to your mind.

_____
_____
_____
_____
_____
_____
_____

Today I will
_____
_____
_____
_____
_____
_____
_____
_____
_____
_____
_____
_____

# DAY 26

Date_____

Proverbs 28:13 (KJV)
He that covereth his sins shall not prosper; but whoso confesseth and forsaketh them shall have mercy.

In your own words, write what this Scripture means to you.

_____
_____
_____
_____
_____
_____

How can you apply this Scripture to your life today?

_____
_____
_____
_____
_____
_____

What have you prayed for and you received it immediately after you prayed?

_____
_____
_____
_____
_____
_____

Pray for 15 - 30 minutes and write any thoughts the Holy Spirit brings to your mind.

_____
_____
_____
_____
_____
_____
_____

Today I will

_____
_____
_____
_____
_____
_____
_____
_____
_____
_____
_____
_____
_____

# DAY 27

Date_____

Psalm 130:1-2 (KJV)

Out of the depths have I cried unto thee, O Lord, hear my voice: let thine ears be attentive to the voice of my supplications.

In your own words, write what this Scripture means to you.

_____
_____
_____
_____
_____
_____

How can you apply this Scripture to your life today?

_____
_____
_____
_____
_____
_____

What have you prayed for and you received it immediately after you prayed?

_____
_____
_____
_____
_____
_____

Pray for 15 - 30 minutes and write any thoughts the Holy Spirit brings to your mind.

_____
_____
_____
_____
_____
_____
_____

Today I will
_____
_____
_____
_____
_____
_____
_____
_____
_____
_____
_____
_____
_____

# DAY 28

Date_____

Acts 20:24 (KJV)

But none of these things move me, neither count I my life dear unto myself, so that I might finish my course with joy, and the ministry, which I have received of the Lord Jesus, to testify the gospel of the grace of God.

In your own words, write what this Scripture means to you.

_____
_____
_____
_____
_____
_____
_____

How can you apply this Scripture to your life today?

_____
_____
_____
_____
_____
_____

What have you prayed for and you received it immediately after you prayed?

_____
_____
_____
_____
_____

Pray for 15 - 30 minutes and write any thoughts the Holy Spirit brings to your mind.

___

Today I will

___

# DAY 29

Date_____

Joel 2:13 (KJV)

And rend your heart, and not your garments, and turn unto the Lord your God: for He is gracious and merciful, slow to anger, and of great kindness, and repenteth him of the evil.

In your own words, write what this Scripture means to you.

_____
_____
_____
_____
_____
_____

How can you apply this Scripture to your life today?

_____
_____
_____
_____
_____
_____

What have you prayed for and you received it immediately after you prayed?

------------------------------
------------------------------
------------------------------
------------------------------
------------------------------
------------------------------

Pray for 15 - 30 minutes and write any thoughts the Holy Spirit brings to your mind.

_____
_____
_____
_____
_____
_____
_____

Today I will

_____
_____
_____
_____
_____
_____
_____
_____
_____
_____
_____

# DAY 30

Date_____

Romans 1:7b (KJV)
Grace to you and peace from God our Father, and the Lord Jesus Christ.

In your own words, write what this Scripture means to you.

_____
_____
_____
_____
_____
_____
_____

How can you apply this Scripture to your life today?

_____
_____
_____
_____
_____
_____

What have you prayed for and you received it immediately after you prayed?

_____
_____
_____
_____
_____
_____

Pray for 15 - 30 minutes and write any thoughts the Holy Spirit brings to your mind.

_____
_____
_____
_____
_____
_____
_____

Today I will

-----------------------------------------------
-----------------------------------------------
-----------------------------------------------
-----------------------------------------------
-----------------------------------------------
-----------------------------------------------
_____
_____
_____
_____
_____
_____
_____

## Contact

The Walk of Faith Journals are available wherever books ae sold. To order copies from the author or to inquire about the author doing book signings, speaking, or ministering at your event, please contact her at:

bowilliams1969@gmail.com

www.ingramcontent.com/pod-product-compliance
Lightning Source LLC
Chambersburg PA
CBHW051432290426
44109CB00016B/1528